The Night Marsh

Also by Penny Harter

Along River Road
Buried in the Sky
Lizard Light
Turtle Blessing
Grandmother's Milk
Shadow Play: Night Haiku
Stages and Views
At the Zendō
The Monkey's Face
The Price of Admission
In the Broken Curve
Hiking the Crevasse
White Flowers in the Snow
Lovepoems
The Orange Balloon

The Night Marsh

Poems

Penny Harter

WordTech Editions

Published by WordTech Editions
P.O. Box 541106
Cincinnati, OH 45254-1106

ISBN: 9781933456973
LCCN: 2007943655

Poetry Editor: Kevin Walzer
Business Editor: Lori Jareo

Visit us on the web at http://www.wordtechweb.com

Acknowledgements

The author is grateful to Michael Lustbader for the front cover image, which originally appeared in his book *Butterfly Dreams: The Seasons through Haiku and Photographs*, published by Natural Tapestries, and to William J. Higginson for the back-cover photograph.

The author is grateful to the editors and publishers of the journals and books listed below, in which the following poems, sometimes in slightly different forms, first appeared:

American Nature Writing 2001 (Oregon State University Press): "Night Drive."
Blueline: "Going Home."
Buried in the Sky (La Alameda Press, 2001): "Mirage, December 1999," "Night Drive," "Sometimes the Snow."
Contemporary American Voices: "Peat Bog Woman," "Elephant Heaven."
Eden Waters: "Sometimes Late at Night."
The Edison Review: "Feeding the Horses in Texas."
Exit 13: "Ripples."
Grandmother's Milk (Singular Speech Press, 1995): "Absence," "No Enemy," "Your Last Words."
ISLE: "Each Green Thing," "The Night Marsh," "Night Drive."
Lips: "Face."
Middle Jersey Writers (Middlesex County [NJ] Arts Council, 1979): "On the Mountain."
Spindrift (Northwind Publishing, 2006): "Seasons of Our Wounds."
The Price of Admission (From Here Press, 1986): "Beneath the Stars."
Tiferet: "A Promise of Home," "Within the Dark," and "Where the Others Are"; and "One Moonless Night" (in *Tiferet* on-line).

Umbrella: "The Wall at the End of the World," "Below the Trees," "The Oracle."
U. S. 1 Worksheets: "Ghost Story."
Valparaiso Poetry Review: "Archaeology."

for Bill
who has loved through it all with me

Contents

III   The Night Marsh

The Night Marsh

I

Archaeology

Archaeology

She is always unearthing something—
here, a rotting bone a dog buried,
there, a headless doll with
stuffing leaking from its chest.

She digs in this field each night,
sniffing the dirt, savoring the strata
as she claws her way down
through soil and clay.

Perhaps the grinning skulls
of her cursed father, mother,
will turn up, blind as bulbs
waiting to sprout into her palms.

She carries resurrection in her hands,
her fingers splayed to sift the earth,
searching for some fragment of a skull
that answers to her name.

Peat Bog Woman

1.

She had red hair.
She has red hair,
a wild bloom still sprouting
from her leather scalp.

She is stained brown,
her face a hard raisin,
her eyelids ridged closed.

I would touch her breasts—
one tilts up, the other down,
no longer twins
humming in harmony.

She died in her early thirties.
She sank on her back.
She was pressed by the bog
for two thousand years.

She died in her early thirties.
On the laboratory table
their gloves brush peat
from her face.

She sank on her back.
She has red hair.
Carefully, they wash it
strand by strand.

Scraps of faded linen
stick to her stomach
under clasped hands that curl
like claws and meet at her navel.

Her arms bridge her torso,
an arc from there to here,
her red hair—a forest of fire.

2.

If they scrape cells
from the inside of your cheek
and carry them away,
the cells will know
when you touch that place again,
will shiver if it hurts.

And if they probe the mouth
of Peat Bog Woman, find a tongue
and scrape from it her cells,
will her children millennia away
cry out in recognition?

At night in the museum
her body lies in a glass coffin,
preserved like the bones of a saint.

Dust settles on the things
we think we ought to keep.
She has red hair, a galaxy
streaming from the promise
of her head, the cradle
of her flesh. Red hair.

Frijoles Canyon, New Mexico

She climbs a wooden ladder
against the cliff face, crawls
into the shadows of a cave.

She curls against an inner wall
her belly dark with longing.
"Soon, little one, soon,"
the wind growls
as it licks the cave mouth.

The sky rumbles
as she scratches more clouds
into the soot-stained walls,
but the rain does not come.

Blessing Dream, Santa Fe

What animal gave me its ear
last night, loved me enough
to lick it deep into the hinge
of my jaw?

My fingers found it,
softly furred at the rim,
angled below my right temple.

The ear was black inside, smelled
of cinnamon and cloves, opened
into a rocky den the wind scoured
as we slept, the beast and I,
on some mountainside.

Awake, now, I trace where
the ear was grafted to my head,
search the mirror. Morning
rustles the cottonwood leaves
outside my window, and I
remember the black rattle
that came before the ear,
the gourd I have been running from,
its furred wings still on the table,
its sharp face waiting to sing.

Voices

Voices crackle in my sleep
like some far off wireless
left on, gone awry, radioing
to its echo.

I search the long blind tunnel of the dream.
My ear opens slowly, an old wound
pulling apart, the scab breaking
as faded faces, their sepia tints
bleeding into one another
begin to move, to speak.

What party is gathered around a bonfire
blowing broken chords into a night of harmonicas?
Who calls my name again and again
from a path of rocks under the waterfall?

I feel my tongue swallow
the saliva of my dream speech,
my vocal chords flex,
and I am keening soundlessly,
"Here I am. I am here!"

"What?" they answer. "Who?"

Each Green Thing

Each green thing
that pushes up through dark earth,
sends out tendrils for roots,
and breaks free, raising
its head into the sky—

each green thing,
whether in garden or forest,
even the weed by road's edge,
does not care what name
we give it, knows only

the mineral taste of water,
the power of wind,
the manna of sunlight falling
wave after wave upon the fragile
spiral of its days,

while our need to label
the living and the dead, says

Catch it, bind it in a net of names,
and then we'll understand
who we are.

Harvest Home

Last night I cradled
a gathering of corn, my arms
heavy with gold, my lap
warm as an abundant field.

I wanted to give it away,
share the harvest
with any hungry animal,
I had so much.

Soon shadows came
to take some from my hands,
and then the gentle cows
whose brows were white as milk.

Afterward, I sought the stars
and the rows that led to them,
dark furrows lapping my feet
with the promise of sleep

while behind me, discarded husks
lifted on the evening wind
and fell again to earth.

Sometimes Late at Night

Sometimes late at night
when the dark lifts me from my bed,
I float in it, and all the bodies of my life—
my own, yours, the dear shapes of my parents
over dinner, the sturdy flesh of my children—
seem insubstantial, floating beside me
in that dark, gone to smoke or mist.

Even this planet, rolling through the greater dark
where gaseous fires sputter and go out,
grows wraith-like, a hologram
I poke my finger through as I drift beside it,
unable to find my way home,
because home doesn't matter anymore,
because home makes a sound like the wind.

A Promise of Home

to welcome a visitor

If it falls from the stars and comes to your door,
extending black, segmented limbs in hesitant
greeting, or banging them together in a gesture
you recognize as supplication;

if it makes a noise like autumn crickets
or dry leaves scraping in the night wind,
yet has no hole for mouth, as you know mouth,
but sends that rasp from somewhere deep
inside its fragile, shining thorax;

and if it has no eyes, as you know eyes,
for you to see inside its soul, but bows,
bobbing its triangular head like a bud
on a tender stem, will you know how
to receive this unthinkable visitation?

Perhaps the lemon yellow light will call it
down to your front porch, that globe hanging
from the ceiling that glows with a promise
of home, of siblings clustered on the couch,
and food, and maybe love.

If you are lucky, it will come to you,
and you must tender it your animal hand
as you would to a strange dog, letting him sniff
to learn that you're okay, you're not afraid,
and see—his tail is wagging now—
he will not bite because he trusts you,
and you trust him.

And if you let it in your house, extend
the blessing that you know it needs
in this place very far from what it knows
as home, creation will begin again,
setting itself ablaze in the dark.

Multiple Exposures

Sometimes we slide sideways
until faint shimmers vibrate
at the edges of our flesh,
promising escape,

or we may slip upwards,
find translucent haloes
eager to crown our skulls
with temporal salvation.

Even our pet dogs who trot along,
noses homing on the stream of things,
have ghostly companions
who strain at the same leash
and raise their legs in the same direction,
paws never touching the sidewalk
as the sun spills through their bones,

and the selves that bleed ahead of us,
threatened by the ones who hug our heels
and fill our wakes with phosphorescent sand,
are the demons of each wave's destination,
so greedy to get us there
              that they tug us free
                      from where we are.

Traveling Across the Tundra

Traveling across the great tundra
west of Hudson Bay,
an Eskimo heaps stone upon stone
until the pile is his own height,
then trudges on until
he can no longer see the stone man
and must build another to comfort him.

I see his sun-burnt face,
eyes squinting across the earth's shining
curvature, returning again and again
to the shape he loves.

Who now picks his way across the tundra
looking back to where we stand silently,
all facing the same direction
as he slips down the horizon?

The Wall at the End of the World

The animals got there first—
the buck who tried to leap over
and fell, bloodied, at its base,
then rose to limp back toward us;
the crow who climbed the dark
until her wings broke,
until she dropped like a stone in our path;
and the others, rats and rabbits,
great whales and starfish—
all those we met coming back,
their eyes without reflection.

Still, though, we keep climbing.
For us it will be different.
Are we not just a little lower
than the angels on the other side?

Half-Life

Some physicists say we are blinking
on/off, on/off, always this rhythm of
here/not-here, here/not-here . . .
whatever *here* is . . . along with
the whole flickering show,

like we're foam on a wave
that wants to be particle wanting
to be wave, foam that knows nothing,
only scurries for its life like those
poor blind mice, that trinity made flesh
running after the farmer's wife
until chop-chop her carving knife—
its sharp blade melting even then
into a stew of tails and ore and gone
and there again.

We sputter into metaphor, mutter words
like *universe, quantum, cosmos, chaos*—
those spells our tongues have learned to shape
against the thing that has no name
we visit now and then

in the wind of no place where we live
only half our lives, or live out our half-lives,
racing toward some finish line that isn't
after all.

Your Face Before You Were Born

1.

Well into her eighties, my mother reported,
You're still you, only you look into the mirror
and wonder who that is.

Who are the transients in our bodies,
trying them on like snakes do patterned skin
before the shedding?

Long ago I hurtled down a chute
like a child on a polished slide,
left behind familiar fields of starlight
as I tumbled headfirst into hay
or whatever soft grass received me—
a dream I still revisit in the dark.

It's raining today, and I wonder
whether rain dreams as it cycles
through us, becoming blood, lymph,
urine, saliva, tears.

2.

After each meal in the zendō,
we scraped what was left into
a communal wooden bowl,
a daily offering set out for birds
or forest animals—no morsel
should be wasted.

To go back, they say,
we travel through a tunnel
as if reentering the womb
and find, beyond the flesh,
a brilliance left behind.

When our flesh breaks down,
cells to molecules to atoms,
into a distance we have not yet mapped,
what is not wasted,
         and what is given back?

Diffusion

If I leave my body,
can I burrow beneath the dirt,
become a blind, segmented tube
that eats and excretes as I turn the soil,
crumbs marking my passage?

If I leave my body,
can I enter the crystals of water
in a winter lake becoming ice,
lose myself in flowing or freezing,
un-amazed at the singular shapes
I now assume?

Today, a blizzard beckons,
the swirling flakes moaning
diffuse, diffuse,
as I press my hands to the cold glass
and my white bones answer.

Leftover Snow

Alien, this white stuff
from the sky, now ragged
hills by the side of the road.

Find that old photograph
of you as a child, planted
beside some giant drift
that dwarfs you.

Remember the igloos you built,
the snowmen you rolled into life
from the only water there ever was
or will be.

Here's that snow again,
but you have not recycled yet.

Snow lasts, reluctant
to let go of its monologue
that evens all things out
and weights old limbs,
that catalogs our passing
and forgets.

Below the Trees

Sleet strikes black windows.
Ice shines in the trees.
                    Below the trees
beneath dead leaves, our cat lies
frozen, dead now for some weeks.

When we touched her in her bed,
her body was an unexpected loaf
of something heavier than bread.
Her fur felt stiff, her paw like that
of some stuffed thing.

Talk to me of dust returned to dust,
of flesh to dirt. Talk to me about
the way the sun sets early and the dark
holds on.

Groundhog Skull

Groundhog, your skull is yellowed,
baked dry and etched with cracks
from seasons above ground.
It fits the cradle of my palm
as my thumb strokes your death.

Your skull is a glyph, a map
to the interior of bone we share—
scaffolding for our mutual meat.

Your curved tusks that dug
into the safety of the dark
now probe the empty air,
and your vacant eye sockets stare
as my fingers push through
into the sky.

I remember you waddling
in the weeds beside the tracks,
slow-moving beast who tunneled up
to blindly greet the sun.

Perhaps you dream of me now
as I do of you, as I burrow into
the moist night where my ancestors live,
sifting their dirt between the splayed digits
of my paws.

Ghost Story

Although you crave it, the story frightens you,
pulls you into dark hallways, cobwebbed passages,
crumbling buildings where blood stains the floor
and screams echo from dense corners.

When you look in the mirror, a transparent face
floats just behind and over your left shoulder,
mouthing questions you will never answer.
A midnight phone call offers only static.

In bed, you pull up the scant protection
of sheet and blanket, close your eyes to hide
from whatever might shimmer by your feet
in a vaguely human shape.

But later, surfacing from sleep, you know
that something came to you, the dream receding
like a hand your hand remembers, its bony knuckles
dear and familiar in the chill before sunrise.

Reading the Signs

In ancient times
they read the cracks in bones,
the markings on a shell,
or movement of the stars
to learn how it would be.

Today, I split a boneless chicken breast,
rip it apart along a translucent seam,
and cast strings of fat into the sink.

What can I discern
about the days and years ahead
in this new constellation?

The Oracle

The oracle wears the whiskered face
of an unknown animal, peers out at us
on autumn evenings, its eyes glowing
from tangles of weeds and roadside trash,
from the fringes of vacant city lots,
from patches of woods we've left untouched
to grace our lavish lawns.

Its teeth are sharp, white warnings in the dark,
and may provoke the cries that startle us
awake from what we call our sleep.

The oracle predicts without speaking,
slaps its tail for emphasis, eludes our traps.
It knows we are bigger than it is,
has learned that we don't care to heed
the messages it brings us from the deep.

Those who have chosen to stand watch
beside some unkempt border where it's been
say they have seen the trail it leaves behind,
as it flattens the undergrowth on its way home.

And those who dare to follow its faint path,
claim they hear a keening in the grass,
a sorrow in the rustling leaves,
a cradle song that's always just beyond
in the unrelenting night.

This Prayer

It is always dark in this prayer,
a dark that seals our eyes.

Black stones are words
in this prayer, held in the dark
of folded hands that let them go

out where the universe curves
into itself and labors.

Night Drive

We are driving, the only sound
the hiss of tires on pavement,
a steady rain, the highway
winding through black hills.

Sometimes fields stretch to the horizon
where between long hours of wet road
we see a distant farmhouse blink
and go out as we leave it behind.

Suddenly a light streaks down the sky,
burning so brightly as it dies
that it seems not there at all,
something huge and silent that slashes
the dark like a knife, and is gone.

We keep on driving, our destination
a motel we'll find along the way,
while I almost remember that rift
in the night, my dumb finger seeking
its shape in my palm.

Imilac Meteor

Held up to the sky, this sliver glows,
its crystalline layers flickering
as if they were still gaseous,
lit by interior light.

In its patterns, see a bird in flight,
or an amber animal that sleeps
between iron-nickel wings—
random shapes cut out and polished,
given to the air.

Look how they mirror back to us
the density of flesh, that mesh
of molecules that maps our lives
until we fuse with earth or fire
while orbiting the sun.

II

Gossamer

Gossamer

Somewhere in this garden
a spider is spinning
transparent gossamer,
the rooms I have lost.

I tell her, "Spin well, my dear.
Loose tensile thread
from that tiny gut
you will never empty

until you've gone to spider dust,
given to the wind."

Somewhere in this garden
blueprints that faded and died
in my lost rooms, hang on a strand
between rose bushes

absorbing the color of the sky
as I walk through.

Ghosts

What hand traced the ammonites
etched in these mountain stones,
then laid across their spirals tiny fronds,
delicate tendrils caught in a strange wind?

Wandering on the gravel road
through the woods of my childhood,
I often stooped to finger bits of shale,
seeking those that held the ghosts of ferns.

The pen that writes these words will also last—
plastic artifact pointed in some landfill toward
our own extinction, like a compass needle

Ripples

Out there is the pond
that all things enter,
and we plunge after them,
doing the crawl,
raising arm over arm,
drawing breath after breath
from the alternating air.

Our things slowly spiral
out of reach, the ripples
from their entry going flat,
the waves from our kicking feet
never reaching shore.

See how that old TV flickers
as it drowns, its faces gasping,
its volume slowly sinking
bit by bit as it broadcasts
down the path of its escape

from the density of signals
it won't translate anymore,
from the remote triggers
in our outstretched hands.

Strawberries and Cream

Long ago your lover brought you
strawberries and cream,
a small offering placed before you—
ripe strawberries, thick cream.

You never told me her name.
You only told me, wonder in your voice,
that she loved you so much
she brought you strawberries and cream.

You had other lovers.
The years are clouds, dust motes
floating in rooms of afternoon sun.

Now you are dead.
Strawberries and cream.
If she is not dead,
she is old.

Does she remember
the taste of your kisses?
The empty bowl?

In That Other World

In that other world, the dead roost in trees,
watch us with eyes scattered as leaves.

The sun or some far star feeds them still
as they rock on the wind that carried them.

In that other world, the dead breathe in unison,
exhaling molecules that home on ours

as we ride beside them in the flimsy nests
of our lives, waiting to be fed.

Memories of Birds

The mourning doves who were building
their nest on the fire escape
have given up.

Mornings, we watched him bring twigs,
tenderly mount her back
to tuck his offerings around her.

She sat on almost nothing
as they worked, just cold metal slats
and the spaces between,

but she believed in nest,
and each time he brought more,
she nestled down to shape the round.

Now their half-woven circle
of bent twigs holds only rain
and memories of birds,

and we are the shadows who moved
across the window, our voices
neither bird nor wind;

who wanted to witness
the intimate acts of their lives—
and they said no.

Of Beak and Blood

A friend gave me an angel,
black icon atop an iron rod
that supports a votive candle
in a circle of iron.

The angel is small, her head round.
No features grace her face,
though her robed arms are open
as if in benediction above the flame
that I will never light.

To honor my guardian, I have made an altar,
stuck a trinity of feathers into the space
between the holder and its white candle.

The first, serrated beige and brown,
seems fallen from some hawk's wing.
The second is a striped and fluffy shaft
from a fledgling raptor's breast,
and the dark spine of the third
separates black from gray—
night from day.

Ringing the candle, these feathers
bear memories of beak and blood
which I offer to this angel, hoping
she can taste them on her iron tongue.

Pain

Pain burns like votive candles
in a niche reserved for the Virgin
or some other icon,
flickering red and yellow;

burns like birthday candles
in the muscle of the mind,
that convoluted baby
curled up around itself
and confident of being.

When you blow out the candles
make a wish.

Winter Count

A Winter Count depicts important events
in Native American tribal life each year.

In last night's dream I held
between thumb and index finger
of each hand, the pale wing of a moth.

Powder stained my fingertips
like dust, as I opened that symmetry
into the light.

Now I let the insect go, still tethered
to my heart, that calendar of blood,
and watch it beat its wounded wings
to yet another Winter Count.

Seasons of Our Wounds

What seasons
haunt the wounds of the flesh,
the spasms of the heart?

Scars heal too slowly, years
crawling toward the time
when pain sleeps in our cells
and we forget the original betrayals.

Inflammation lingers, red
around the edges of our wounds,
while cold in the mouth
of the sky breathes us blue.

Internal stitches dissolve,
and nesting birds gather hair
we've dropped along the way.

Perhaps it's all spring in the end,
what we think lost, sprouting
again and again out of the dirt
to startle us.

Your Last Words

When they blew into my window
I did not recognize your last words
that first bloomed among the roses,

and the shape of your mouth,
that startled welcoming of death
in the garden, had changed too,
so I did not recognize the words
as blossoms from your lips.

So strange had they become
from the weather of years
that when they arrived,
your last words,
I only knew it was spring again,
and the fragrant wind
awakened me.

No Enemy

There is no enemy among the roses
beside our sidewalk though their petals
shrivel brown like dried blood
in the slant winter sun.

And there is no enemy
in the black ice that hides
on our street after twilight rain.

Only the long sigh of the wind
tells us that night is coming
over the hills like a train
with no eyes, whistling faintly
from so far away
we can't tell if that stain
around it in the sky is smoke
or angels.

Wings and Shadows

What of angels, if there be angels?

Coat hangers untwist in Mother's hands
to be reshaped for my two oaktag wings.

What of the storm in this room?

Feathers circle my head—
a whirlwind sent by God
while faithful Mother labors
to catch and glue them in place.

And do I then, rapt in white, ascend?

Snow falls heavily outside
and someone rises into it.

And why do I think now of bats
opening their webbed membranes
to the night, sailing overhead as if
they were ashes from dead stars?

And why do all wings have shadows?

If there be angels, let them descend
from their nests of dark matter
to meet me.

The Melting Snow

1.

It is nineteen-twenties snow,
stubbornly clinging to weathered wood
but melting in patches, run-off darkening
the boards of the old porch steps.

Someone has already swept the porch.
Three young children sit on the top stair,
holding hands. Their heads step down
from left to right in the morning light.

My aunt, the youngest, wears a felt
baker's hat matching her smocked coat
with fabric buttons, beneath which
in her forties she will lose a breast,
and then the rest.

My uncle is all in wool, a watch-cap
pulled below his ears, the coat collar up.
He does not smile, but gazes straight ahead
into years that promise a demented wife,
a failing heart.

My mother, the oldest, squints into the sun
and smiles with closed lips.
A fleecy hat covers her forehead;
the lamb collar of her coat curls up,
to meet her chin-length, dark hair.

She looks off to the side, toward a horizon
she can not imagine—a husband whose collision
with a truck will, in her old age, take her life.

2.

Behind these three, the house number
gleams on frosted glass, the handle
of a snow shovel leans against the door
above the front end of a sled on its side,
and a child-sized wooden chair sits
empty over my mother's right shoulder.

There are patterns in this photograph:
the angle of the shovel on the door
like a minute-hand just before noon;
the slanted line of the three heads,
youngest to oldest, left to right;
the square toes on black boots,
laces crossing to tie at the ankles;
and the slats on the back of the chair
that echo three gray steps descending
into deeper snow.

And there are ghosts—the dog Jerry
who surely has made paw-prints
in the yard, the children yet to be
who will perch on the same porch
for similar photos, and the missing
parents behind the cameras.

On the other side of the heavy door,
the marble clock on the mantle chimes,
light pours through stained-glass
in the living room, and the coal furnace
shudders on against the coming night
and the cold that will follow.

Lost in the Green Room

Tonight, I am lost in the green room
in my grandparents' house in South Orange,
in the green four-poster bed, high off the floor,
where the doctor comes with a long needle
for bad tonsillitis, and I won't, I won't,
I fight him screaming—they hold me down;

where my fingers make shadow-monsters
on the wall until I hear something scrabbling there.
Squirrels, Mother says, though I think it must be rats
like those in my converted sun-porch room at home
where something heavy ran across my legs at night,
and the traps told the truth.

I am lost in the green room
where I hear coughing, some talk of whooping cough,
glimpse a white nightshirt on a bare-foot child—
it isn't me, though the child runs from the green room.

And someone goes up in a spinning green bed,
rises into the night sky, eyes closed, while Mother reads
"Wynken, Blynken, and Nod"—she loves that poem,
the wooden shoe, the stars, the river of pure delight.
I miss her, want to go there now, but I am lost.

Lost in the green room in my grandparents' house.
Rain fills the gutters outside, and water gurgles
down the drain in the bathroom off the hall
where I stand on a little stool—I can't remember
the teeth-brushing song—white toothpaste splattering
the mirror while Poppy laughs behind me.
All of it lost, lost with the green room.

Once, waking from a nap in the green room,
I left my bed to climb the narrow attic stairs,
pulled the light chain at the top, one bare bulb,
and found a dusty set of books for children.
The first one, with big black print, I carried back
to look at in the green room, and later
found my way to the Land of Oz.

Another time, I opened the musty attic trunk
to try on Nanna's dresses stored inside.
But I couldn't climb into that trunk, couldn't
lay a bunch of white and purple violets
on her irradiated chest. I was not allowed
though I'd picked them from under the hedge
just for her, as she lay dying in her bed
in a room with no color. Not allowed.

Tonight, I am lost in the green room.
Headlights sweep the ceiling, *whoosh, whoosh.*
Luminous exhalations seep through the rafters
to gently rock me in my bed. Rhythmic blessings
drop from a radiant beast on the roof peak,
some guardian come down the dark for me:

Rock-a-bye baby, in the treetop,
When the wind blows, the cradle will rock.

Querying the Dark

1.

Deep in pre-dawn sleep, in the spare bedroom
of my parents' double-wide, we jerk awake
to a rattling doorknob, banging on the door,
and my father's shouting,

It's snowing! Snow! Snow! Wake up!
Wake up! Snow! Come look! Wake up!

We are here, trying to care for this old man,
half-gone with dementia, who wakes early
to wander room-to-room in his dark house
while my mother struggles in the hospital,
gravely injured from the accident he caused.

2.

On an earlier visit, waking at midnight,
I heard my father's muffled voice
as I lay awake, my door cracked open.

What's going to happen to us?

He sounded, then, like a small boy
as he queried the dark around his bed,
the dark of having lived for ninety years,
one eye already blind;

as he queried the growing dark
inside my mother who had now become
his mother, though I was still her child,
straining to hear her reassuring murmurs.

3.

Snow! Snow! It's all white! Wake up!

Rising from the sweet escape of sleep,
I peek through a slit in the blinds
to see a coating on the brittle grass,
but the dark still pushes hard against the dawn,
and I do not open the door.

She Would Not Eat

She would not eat, my mother,
in those days before the end
when we tried to bribe her
with ice-cream and promises
of next summer by the sea.

I just can't, she'd say. *I know
you want me to, but I can't*,
and she'd refuse to swallow,
though she could, as if to stop
her throat against such matter,
such dense weight.

And we did not understand
that she was emptying herself—
was foam spilling through
a pair of old shoes abandoned
at the tide-line, or water returning
from a child's lost pail.

Yet when we asked her
if she wanted to die, she cried
God, no, and hid more food
beneath her pillow, as if
she were covering it with sand.

Another Heaven

Who are they, these strangers
whose sepia faces stare at me
from the faded pages of this album,
its velvet spine long broken?

Where is the heaven they inhabit,
the one that shimmers next to now,
fading in and out, fickle as lightning?

Has my mother entered it,
finding her proper place
among our captive ancestors
whose eyes are enigmatic
as tombstones?

I would slit the doubled pages,
tear them open to expose
the torsos trapped within,

ranks of fleshless bodies
rooted in old glue, their faces
peering out oval windows
cut in spotted cardboard.

Blink, and the edges shift,
the walls waver, and someone
cool as river water comes
to sit on the bed's edge,

to stroke our sleeping limbs
until we swim as we have not done
since the womb.

Rain Tonight

Rain tonight, and the dark
deepens, floating our sleep.

I wake to probe that pool,
let fall a drowsy weight
of arm off the bed's edge
into still waters.

Fathoms down,
a ghost limb quickens,
writhing like seaweed
as it rises.

Its cold fingers drift
between my own, interlacing
in the childhood game
of church and steeple.

And when we open the door,
there's no one there.

Within the Dark

Like those faint stars we cannot see
except that we look straight ahead
and find them flickering at our vision's edge,

our sleeping faces glimmer with each breath,
cast signatures of light above the bed
where every night we give ourselves away.

Some snails leave phosphorescent slime
behind them as they drag across black sand,
or crawl along the garden's muddy path.

Our transient skin, our fragile skulls within,
cast off a radiance that's only seen
by looking slant within the seeded dark.

Even the Grass

for the child of a friend

In last night's dream, a bat
flew out of a cave, opened black
wings to soar above a twilight stream,
then fell back into the ledges
of its body and was still.

And once, in someone else's dream,
a mirror showed nothing,
nothing at all, even when a hand
swept across it gesturing victory,
and a ruined face pressed tears
against the silver surface as if
it were a photographic plate.

Not long ago, a toddler
collapsed on the summer grass
in the midst of play, asked her mother
for her bedtime toy, and held it
against her small face as she said
"Night-night" and died.

Sometimes things are like that.
The sun goes dark in the day,
and even the grass cannot be trusted.

On the Mountain

The woman lost her pitcher down the well.
After the pump broke
and dirty dishes climbed the crusted sink,
and the toilet wouldn't flush the baby's mess.

It was a plastic pitcher, faded
piece from some shower gift.
When the baby toddled out
barefoot on the frozen dirt,
pink robe opening down her nakedness,
the woman let go of the rope
and lost the pitcher down the well.

On the mountain
things freeze up at night.
The pitcher will be in the ice
by morning.

Inside now, her three daughters,
one not right,
huddle watching the TV
where a man's head floats
among the stars of some far galaxy,
his voice calling, calling.

No!
She hadn't meant for it to be this way at all,
loose windows leaking cold
as the sky darkens.
Not this way at all.

The small bird face
of her stunted one
chirps up at her:

I wanna green crayon for the Christmas tree.

A green crayon
The green crayon at the bottom
of the tin.

When the phone rings she answers it,
speaks of the wall that took her husband
to the hospital, the smashed car,
the water pump, the pitcher.

You can come if you like, Momma.
Didn't want to worry you.

Stars rush at her now
from the TV. Her body parts their stream
as a fallen tree divides the water while,
still rooted, it clings to the soil
of the shore.

She hangs up.

The tiny nipple bulbs
on the fake Christmas tree
glow pink and blue.
The socket hisses as she pulls the plug.
She hadn't meant for it to be.

Her daughters are into the gumdrops now,
pressing sugared wreaths onto their fingers,
sucking on them. The baby's mouth glows
moist orange.

Bedtime.
Three under the dirty blanket.

Then the star-man,
the star-man is talking again.

He raises a bony hand beckoning her
across the sill of the TV.

Finishing the gumdrops for company
she follows him home.

Words After Life

1.

Bent in half, I turned
on my side like a spoon
reflecting the light;
my muffled breath
carried me away.

Where are the former stars,
the glory of the night
that shouted hallelujah
over the mountains?
What are they waiting for?

2.

Open the gate to the swimming
and we all rise up like guppies—
faces surfacing, lips smacking
a greedy hello.

Close the gate in the desert
and we jump against the sun
again and again, learning
a long good-bye

3.

Come on, child,
you've been here before—
remember the smell of sour wine,
the taste of old shoe leather?

There's a fair wind
blowing the sails out of port;
hop on, and I'll buy you
a drink you won't forget—
repentance.

4.

Up here where I hang out
empty closets echo from star to star—
no moth balls of remembrance,
not even a grain of dust
contemplating its own immorality.

5.

Light shrinks over the mountains.
A crow pulls it down.
The bones of my cheeks glow red
on your horizon.

Passing Train at Night

The face in the train window,
backlit like a saint, stares
into the dark and rushing trees,

navigates the web of tracks
across empty streets,
the hollows of your eyes.

The face in the train window
gazes up at buildings that flicker
and go out in the wake of its passing,

and you remember riding through the night,
your forehead pressed against the glass
as the long whistle echoes from your skull
like a comet's tail.

Mirage, December 1999

Always just ahead of us, the mirage stretched
across the asphalt, a wet blue promise

shimmering like faces we have seen
pinned to the horizon at twilight,
smiling an ancestral welcome
as they flicker with ancient stars.

Near the winter solstice now,
the rippling heat of summer
has flattened into memory, the miles
it baptized gone stark beneath the sky.

On this horizon, a streak of peach
flames and goes out.

Somewhere, prayer flags flap from a clothesline
strung across millennia, their fabric transparent
in the solar wind

Old Folks at Home

They're building a retirement community in space,
an orbiting leisure-town for senior citizens
who really want to get away from it all.
There will be special rates on the shuttle,
a resident staff of experts on the science of aging.

No row of rocking-chairs will line the lobby.
Visitors will be rare, out of the question most days.
Organized activities, including the study of stars,
weightless games in the circular gym,
and silent meditation before the universe
will eat the hours.

Better than Florida and Arizona put together,
the brochures will say.
And we who can afford it will buy in,
tempted by the unvarying weather
and the spectacular view of the blue planet.

Won't it be satisfying
to live out the productive years remaining to us
so far removed from Earth
that its daily acts do not violate our rotating
sanctuary?

It will be easy to ignore the news from home,
already stale when it reaches us.
Even the children will have to make do
with occasional phone calls crackling across the void.

Instead of contemplating mortal sorrow
we can turn our eyes to the heavens
and understand how young we are.

When we die they will fly us back to Earth
for our funerals, bury us in the family graveyards,
claiming our flesh as their own.
And that is as it should be despite the fantasies
of silver coffins drifting through families of stars,
watched by our friends until they disappear
into interstellar dust.

III

The Night Marsh

The Night Marsh

This is not about frogs,
their rhythmic croaking
from the swampy edges of a pond,

nor is it a landscape
of the hunter and the hunt.

This marsh extends for miles,
water glittering here and there
under starlight.

The sleepers feel their way
as they stumble from wet land to dry.

There is no hand to hold,
no voice dripping like moss
from the trees, singing,

*Come this way
into the darker dreaming of the day.*

Walking on Water

We know it is possible—
one manifestation of God
has done it.

We think there is a recipe for this,
a formula to follow as we sink
into the stone of our selves,

hoping to learn buoyancy,
hoping to alter our molecules,
to recalibrate the atoms that blew
into our cells from the stars,

and then to surface,
our vibrating flesh so light
our weight dissolves in our wake
as we test the water's skin.

One Moonless Night

One moonless night
I could not see my hands
outstretched before my face

though I knew they were still there,
milky extensions from my wrists
gone under the weight of such dark

that I knew my shadow hands
were also lost, searching for the dream
where they would find again
the wind that blows our spirits into light.

Antiphony

Before dawn, small black birds
perch on the highest limbs
of the bare trees by the tracks,
fluffing their feathers to catch
the rising sun.

Talk to the blue blade of the sky,
some say, when your loved ones
have gone ahead, and they hear you,
though they may not answer.

I open the window and lean out
as if I, too, were waiting for the sun,
and call your name into the wind,

and I hear the birds' antiphonal refrains,
feel the furious beating of their hearts
against the cold.

Today Toward Sunset

Today toward sunset, three crows
soared on the late March wind,
calling to one another until it seemed
that one harsh caw braided the space
between them, then fell toward me
through the fading light.

I heeded their cry, almost
caught it in my open mouth
as my head tilted back
and my face found the sky.

And as I slowly raised my arms,
two crows flew together toward the dark
while the third broke rank,
trailing parting caws behind as if
promising something to the others—
and the braid still held.

I thought of you, then,
of how we'd called to one another,
facing the same horizon,
and wondered whether it were you
or I who broke rank, promising.

Going Home

Going home, your eyes close
as you bounce along the rutted road
visiting a landscape you have made
from fragments—

the face of that cow by the fence,
the neon sign on the all-night diner
set against a black wall of pine,

or a parlor filled with voices
you thought you had lost,
a room through which a stream
from your childhood
is mysteriously flowing,

and you step into the current
on the same flat rocks as always,
only their moss grown thicker
over the years.

Feeding the Horses in Texas

for my father

Dad kept yellow corn from the feed store
in a garbage can out behind the shed.
Dawn and dusk, he shoved a rusty scoop
deep into that can, dumping hard kernels
of boyhood memory on the family farm
into a galvanized pail.

Then he sniffed the wind and nickered
until two horses crossed the neighbor's field
to rest their muzzles on the split-rail fence
and talk to him.

And he made more horse noises,
grinning back as they curled floppy lips
to bare big teeth and munch this ritual gift
from an old man lost in his yard
who raised that steel bucket
as if to his own mouth.

My Great Aunts' Player-Piano

The old piano still sounds
though its keys are yellowed
from the oil of Aunt Allie's fingers
long gone to bone;
though its tin piano rolls whirled away
on the same wind that took the house.

A child plays it now,
enters the familiar room in moonlight
faint as the filmy clouds that drift
between the stars, and she remembers
the old songs—

"Down in the valley, the valley so low,
Hang your head over, hear the wind blow."

 "Sleep my child and peace attend thee
All through the night."

"Sweet and low, sweet and low
Wind of the Western Sea . . ."

and even the ragtime
that bounced from her grandmother's hands
one New Year's Eve.

And as the child plays
they listen—the dear dog who curls
beside her feet as they pump the pedals,
the mice that live out on the porch
where Aunt Molly still must sleep
through every kind of weather,

and the faithful dust motes
that were and always will be
suspended in the stream of the child's breath
as she sings along.

Beneath the Stars

In the autumn twilight
the white wicker chair stiffens.
Paint has flaked from its woven body.
Birds have splattered its seat.

The white wicker chair was new once,
sitting across from another white wicker chair,
holding sunlight on white cottons, and laughter
careless as ice-cubes in leftover drinks.

Inside the distant house, lights come on.
Someone laughs, slamming down a window.
A cold wind whispers through wicker cracks;
the chair creaks as it drifts into night.

Tiptoe across the shriveled grass.
Approach the chair quietly.
Curl into its moonlit lap.
Notice the rounded arm rests,
the gentle embrace of the curved back.

Now close your eyes
and listen to a long-ago croquet game
resume beneath the stars.

Dream Dance for Valentine's Day

Offer your heart like the box
you once gave your mother—
red tinfoil glittering, gold letters
simmering as you raised it
to offer chocolate-covered cherries.

Open your heart like a house,
your grandmother's house
with blue tiles on the walls
and stone cradles holding flowers
plucked from the stream below.

Enter your heart like a dream
you crack open in the dark,
and dance with this muscle
that swims so gracefully in place,

an unexpected guest at your party,
a lover you have known for years
whose own mouth opens to join in
before the music ends.

The Neighbors' Windows

1.

The neighbors' windows flicker
through the rain, silent boats
floating among the bare branches
across the railroad tracks.

I darken the rooms where I live,
lean my elbows on the sill,
and open to the waves of autumn.

What shadows move across
those distant lights, waver
in the rising wind?

2.

I'm still a child, staring out
the windows of the car at dusk,
a changeling sending my spirit
into lit houses that we pass
on the way home.

We have gotten Father from the train,
heard the hissing as that huge engine
pulled away in clouds of steam and cinders.

3.

I would line these windows up,
make a tunnel for some train to enter
carrying the living and the dead
through every kind of storm
toward some great house of light.

Where the Others Are

Going. They are going.
They wave from the old photo,
then turn around to leave,
walking hand-in-hand
like a kindergarten class,
down a street you remember,
scuffing their shoes through
puddles, fallen leaves.

Look, a cloud has come
to meet them, and they shimmer
in the doorway of this dream.

But before they go, they turn
to wave at you again, their hands
letting go of everything.

The Hub

1.

We sleep at the center of a great wheel
whose spokes dissolve in galaxies of dust
At the hub of this wheel, we dream
a child's dream of riding a tricycle
round and round, careful not to fall
off the edge of the known world.

And as we sleep, we listen for whispers
falling from dear lips we used to know,
lips that kissed our infant foreheads,
or caressed our mouths, delicately probing
the sweetness.

But if we wake, if we venture out,
we may lose ourselves, our compass
meant for a polarity we have left behind
in our search for the solace of something
beyond a human face.

Yet we may still find kindred in that dust,
and names etched in stone to hold them still.

2.

It is a family graveyard we will stray into,
but in the woods beyond the old stone wall
a deer leaps, its white tail flickering in the dark,
a dandelion puff dispersing stars
beneath the flames of autumn trees,

and from one blazing branch, a birdhouse
sways in the wind, inviting transients
to fold their wings and shelter for a while,
and we do.

Translating the Sky on the Morning of My Birthday

Here, where it touches the Earth,
the sky hums with traffic—
whistles and bells of a passing train,
a truck revving its engines,
the distant roar of a plane.

Outside my window, birds chirp
in the budding trees as they woo
and build their fragile nests,

and somewhere in the molecules of air
my infant cries reverberate, mixing
with my mother's groans.

In this place where sky begins
wind goes round and round,
and clouds, ephemeral as cells,
touch one another—moist whispers
I can almost hear.

And as I stare at this blue illusion,
this caul that conceals
a sputtering void of gas and fire,
of ice and rock in an infinite dark,

I am untethered, an astronaut
cartwheeling into the abyss,
my arms and legs flailing
like a newborn's.

Elephant Heaven

In the documentary, the scarred old elephant—
kidnapped in her youth from Africa,
then bumped from circus to zoo
when an accident crippled her foot—

after twenty years with none of her kind
is released into a sanctuary where she finds
trees, grasses, gentle hills, and an old friend,
daughter of her heart from their circus days.

And oh, the trumpeting joy of reunion,
the prolonged welcome of twined trunks,
the stroking of one another's flanks,
remembered and beloved in this
elephant heaven on Earth.

Perhaps that's how it will be for us
after long isolation in the zoos of our flesh
when our chains are removed, and we exit
the cage, moving fearfully down the ramp,
dazed and blinking, into the verdant landscape
of our dreams, an Eden from whose forests
all manner of spirits come to welcome us,
their cries in every language of the beasts.

The Green Gaze

Sunlight glancing through the trees
dissolves to dirt.

I meet the green gaze of my cat,
her almost yellow eyes, black-rimmed,
along the path I follow through green ferns
to her gone flesh, her lifeless fur.

She demands love, nudging my ankles
in the old way, thrusting her wet nose
into the palm I lower by her grave
where I stroke rough weeds
into her shape.

It is the eyes we notice first,
those almost human eyes
that meet ours in a space
we seldom recognize as shared

where an inchworm hangs from a leaf,
back and forth across the sun.

Relativity

We move on the Earth
as it moves through us,
keeping pace like the moon does
as we rush along a country road,
its pale circle streaming beside us
through the night.

Thus we stretch the minutes
pointing toward our deaths,
extend the flicker granted
to the molecules that know
the road we're on.

And when we stop in the shadow
of a mountain to catch our breath,
the mountain keeps on going
through the atoms of our flesh.

Penny Harter

Poet and fiction writer Penny Harter has presented readings, talks, and workshops from coast-to-coast at venues such as the Geraldine R. Dodge Poetry Festivals, the Georgia O'Keeffe Museum, the Border Book Festivals, Haiku North America Conferences, and others. She has also led workshops and participated in collaborative writing with other poets several times in Japan.

Harter's poems and short stories have appeared in many periodicals, including *Ark River Review, Blueline, Earth's Daughters, Exit 13, The Edison Literary Review, Ekphrasis, 5 A.M., Gargoyle, Journal of New Jersey Poets, The Kerf, The Ledge, Lips, Madrona, Newsweek* (Japan), *The New York Times, Ninth Decade* (London), *Oyez Review, Pacific Quarterly Moana* (New Zealand), *Purchase Poetry Review, Shaman's Drum, Shearsman* (London), *Tiferet, Sea Stories, U.S. 1 Worksheets, Whiskey Island Quarterly*, and *Wind*. Translations of her poems have been published in Colombia, Croatia, France, Holland, Japan, Korea, and Romania.

Her poetry, fiction, and essays have been published in books and anthologies from a number of publishers, including Andrews McMeel, From Here Press, Fulcrum, Harper Collins, Katydid Books, Kodansha, La Alameda Press, Little Brown, McGraw-Hill, Milkweed Editions, Negative Capability, New Rivers Press, New World Library, Norton, Oregon State University, Sierra Club Books, Simon & Schuster, Singular Speech Press, Sherman Asher Books, Charles E. Tuttle, Rutgers University Press, Teachers & Writers Collaborative, University of Michigan Press, Utah State University Press, Vintage Books, and White Pine Press. Her illustrated book for children, *The Beastie Book: An Alphabestiary,* is forthcoming from Shenanigan Books early in 2009.

Harter is the author, co-author, or co-editor of more than two-dozen books (see a selected list facing the title page of this book), and many of her poems have been read by Marion Roach on Sirius Radio. A number of her poems appear on various Web sites, including her own: http://penhart.2hweb.net.

Harter has received three fellowships in poetry from the New Jersey State Council on the Arts and a fellowship in teaching writing from the Geraldine R. Dodge Foundation. She also received the Mary Carolyn Davies Memorial Award from the Poetry Society of America, and the first William O. Douglas Nature Writing Award in2002. Harter's autobiographical essay appears in *Contemporary Authors Autobiography Series* (1998; reprinted in *Contemporary Authors*, 1999). She is included in Marquis' *Who's Who of American Women.*

Born in New York City, Harter grew up in Staten Island and New Jersey. She graduated from Douglass College and soon began writing poems. She has taught English at public and private high schools and in evening college courses in New Jersey and New Mexico. Between full-time teaching posts, she has worked as a teaching artist in the New Jersey Writers-in-the-Schools program and as writer-in-residence for the Woodbridge Township (NJ) Schools, serving grades K-12. After more than a decade in Santa Fe, New Mexico, she and her husband, poet and translator William J. Higginson, recently returned to New Jersey, where she continues teaching. Currently, she is a teaching artist with the New Jersey Writers Project sponsored by the New Jersey State Council on the Arts and Playwrights Theatre of New Jersey, and works with a number of private writing students.

CPSIA information can be obtained at www.ICGtesting.com
Printed in the USA
LVOW08s0115170314

377629LV00002B/499/P

9 781933 456973